Preface

An anthology of epic lyrical poems about love
and life, and a reminder that proceeding with
love, kindness, compassion and empathy should
always take precedence for all living beings,
human and animal.

Be Epic, Choose Love.

Soar with the eagles, have the peace of a dove,
there's an infinite source of love which comes
from above. It's within you, it's within me, love is
a beautiful capacity for all of us, you see.

Choose wisely, choose all of the good that's meant to be. Be Epic, Choose Love.

By Lisa J. Pellegrene

Be Epic. Choose Love.

Sunshine

Today I walked past a mirror a

and what did I see?

Eyes with infinite love and wisdom staring back at me.

A heart filled with love, thousands of inspiring stories yet to be told.

My question, will I get to tell them before I get old?

Much sadness, yet joy. All intertwined together as one, I'm thankful for the person I've become. I've shined like a diamond, glistening bright,

I've been humbled and suffered, few knowing my plight. I've talked and I've listened, I've learned and I've shared,

I've overcome struggles, some that most wouldn't dare.

I'm thankful you see, gratitude is present deep within me.

I've learned to dig deep for true beauty within, to know that there's more, I must win.

Win is said loosely - it's not winning at all, it's to know that I am living life giving it my all-

to make life better, it's not just me that is involved.

It's for those whom I love, and it's for all you see, the many sentient beings who I see clearly.

Love is the answer, for all of the good that's meant to be.

To feel I use my gifts and talents to be uplifting to
others,

in a world where so many keep score. What life is
truly about includes love and appreciating the
gift of life more.

It's about love and kindness I say, true strength
from deep inside.

It's the only way I know to be, and also how all can find their way.

The way to truth is to give it our best, to lift up and inspire. Life isn't a test.

It's to spend time with loved ones, to live and to learn, uplift through encouragement and to do our very best to always discern.

Quite a life I've led thus far.

There's been sunshine and heartbreak, the best days and worst days; yet good does prevail, as there is the presence of love which I've learned through it all.

A foundation so strong that no one can break. It's love so strong that it can survive an earthquake.

It's a fact of life that I know now. While others may worry about the smallest of things, I know better, there is love through it all.

Life is a gift, much too valuable to argue or fret.

Each day is a gift, so live it that way so that there are no regrets.

Live life, and love with all of your heart, for that's just the start...

of a beauty so deep that is found within one's heart.

Born into this world and given a beautiful start. I just wish all in the world would take heart.

Love one another, don't squabble or fight; rather have love for all humans and animals with all of your might. The strength among us, it's all from within - the soul and the spirit, a heart based in love.

There truly is no greater gift from above, like how God had it planned to teach nothing but love.

A man on a beach I encountered before, spoke gently to me when he saw a sad seeming girl.

It was that day more than a decade ago, I was walking the boardwalk in San Diego.

This human angel, an old man I crossed paths with that day said to me, "Miss do you understand? There's so much within you that's beautiful to all who can and know how to clearly see."

"The lesson you need really isn't from me. I'm just a messenger from heaven maybe.

He said miss don't you see? Here's how it is; the truth you must know.

You're heaven and earth; such as the brightest of stars that light up each night, you're meant to shine bright all of your years, please understand this and it's this that you must see.

Sometimes in the world it seems to be not so easy. Yet, you must remember the importance of this message, as it paves the way for the beautiful life that will be.

You mustn't fret or give in to sadness, as that's not what's meant to be.

Your splendor, your beauty, and your heart - it's pure gold.

You must remember there's some who haven't learned to see another's heart ever so clearly, but that's not about you and that's not about me.

I pray they learn before they grow old, it's up to them how that unfolds. Seeing beauty ever so clearly and choosing love, it's what's meant to be.

The lesson for you is that there's something that you must learn to see. The look in your eyes, so light and so bright, enough to light up the darkest of nights. A beauty, much deeper than most in the world can clearly see in all its delight.

A being of pure love and tranquility. She's funny, she's happy, her talents profound, and she has this ability to bring happiness to others in leaps and bounds.

A smile so precious it's simply divine - a smile that stays with you longer than the finest wine stays fine.

True strength based in love and light, a being you must learn to profoundly see."

He was speaking to me.

For then there's not so much heartbreak or suffering, there's a beauty so profound within you preparing you for all of the good and love, that is what's meant to be.

The struggles, the pain, the heartbreak that you endured, it's because you were learning don't you see.

The struggles prepared you to live a life filled with joy and tranquility and through who you are and who you will continue to be, you will inspire many to clearly see.

You must learn to see yourself clearly and all of the beauty that you hold deep inside. This is your responsibility; and from then on, life is as beautiful as it's meant to be.

I know that the message was meant for me, yet I also believe it's for everyone, you see. Once I realized the message I heard, and understood it profoundly, I thought to myself, others should hear it too, it is also what's meant to be.

This message of love and truth, it's not just for me.

It's for others too, so each can see the beauty and love, it starts with you too.

It's what's meant to be, and the love - that is what is true.

We are all beautiful, don't you see? So please take a moment to understand and see your beauty, truth, and authenticity. The love you also hold deep within represents the most beautiful you.

See your beautiful self, and share this message with me. I want to help others also to clearly see the beauty and the light which is within me that I clearly see - I can also see the beauty and love in you, so very clearly.

I shine my light bright so that others can see that the beauty and light is within all of us. Choose love, and it will be.

See your beauty and love so divine, choose it and you will not fall. You will soar and that will be all. Love takes one far, it's brighter than the brightest of stars.

Choose love, shine bright, you will learn to see all of the beauty and the love that's meant to be.

You are beauty and love. Back to the "human angel" as he said to me…. "There's one thing left to learn to clearly see. See yourself clearly; you must never forget - choose all of the beauty and love within. Then, shine your light bright to live a life with joy and love, that is what's meant to be."

I share this message today to remind you that the beauty and love it's within you too, and it's within me.

It's within all of us, all come into this world born out of love.

Choose love always, it's what's meant to be.

Life is an amazing gift, don't you see? Beauty, love, kindness and compassion, this is meant to be.

And today, I look in the mirror and see eyes filled with infinite love and wisdom staring back at me.

I see love. I see past pain. I see knowledge. I see hope. I see someone who at times fought to live my life and during other times, fought to live - because life is a gift.

There's so much beauty for you and me. I see strength, the truest of true strength. Strength is love, it's clear to see.

I see heartbreak so profound, heartbreak which stung so deep; yet, I mostly see one who overcame heartbreak, to rise above and shine.

One who chooses love, this is how we thrive. Figuratively, you must dive into life, and by this I mean live your life authentically. When you choose love, as it's always what is meant to be; quite frankly, it's how to stay as one with the divine. Love - it's how you stay fine.

Yes, I see my bright shining light, one who overcame, who stands strong with love because I hold onto joy and hope and love with all my might, of these very worthy things I will never lose sight.

Love from above and found within, the choices I make, I choose love. It's how I shine my light.

So come what may, love is here to stay.

I know that we will be alright.

Choose love with all of your might. Love is here for all to see and to be.

Love is the greatest gift and one's most important capacity.

A thousand inspiring stories yet to tell ..a light still so bright that it continues to shine all day and night. I rise above ..I fight the good fight with love in this precious gift called life. Yes, it's always worth prevailing and overcoming any strife in life. The rain may come, yet it does not stay.

Just remember to choose love today, and everyday, and again and again. Love is the answer, love shall win.

Have you ever sat outside on a clear moonlit night? Stared up at the stars and the moon glowing bright? Or sat in the sun with the warm breeze brushing against your skin, in all its delight? Do you stop and look at the flowers in all of their splendor, or enjoy the beauty of nature and all of its might? If you do, then you know, all is alright. It's better than that - this life is a gift and your future is bright.

Adversity is present at times in our life, yet it's what makes us strong. Do not let it break you down, it's not meant to - you see. You're created to stand strong and overcome adversity. This is when you use your God given gifts to rise above, taking you to much better days in this life. You pray, you stand up and fight with love - this takes you to better days. Stay strong in this life with a foundation of love, and you will most definitely be more than alright.

When one falls down, you get back up, no it's not just about winning the Stanley cup. Although, those who do, use their gifts to rise up.

We all have them you see, God gave each of us gifts and talents, present in each of us.

Our talents and gifts bring us joy. So please don't be coy, use your gifts and talents to inspire today. Start with you, and your enthusiasm will inspire all in your view.

Our gifts bring joy, starting with you and all around you too. Our passions ring true in all we do, when we use our gifts remembering to stay true. Remember to choose love and kindness in all that you do. You must remember this, it's true.

Use your gifts and talents as we are all meant to - Be Epic, Choose Love. You too have a light found deep within; you are meant to shine it bright, with love.

Live a life you truly do love, and choose to stand tall with love, with all of your might. I stand for love, I stand for hope.

....These days I'm never one to mope, not that I was, as I knew long ago - I will never lose hope. Hope is your friend. Hope gets you through. It will bring the happiest, most authentic love-based you back again; and again and again, and the time after that.

It's infinite you see, just like love, hope is meant to be.

Life's too special to spend in strife or sadness. Some can't see, but they aren't yet based in reality. Life's a gift. Profoundly and beautifully, a gift.

Realize this and you too will see, a beautiful life exists in the here and now - it is what is meant to be.

Into this world with utmost love, you must choose the peace of a dove. Start with you. Love with all of your heart, it's a gift from above. When I see it in me, I see it in you, a beauty so bright; we need to always stay true.

Stay true to you, and choose love. Be who you are. Your authentic self lights up the night, and brightens each day. Just be you, and always stay true.

The light and the love found deep within, it's the greatest, so bright. When you choose love, you're always alright.

When I looked in the mirror I had something to say. The lesson I get it, it's all so clear now.

After all the adversity and struggle and plight, that light deep within is still shining so bright. Maybe brighter you see, it's a beautiful reality.

I see struggles and pain and wisdom galore, so much knowledge and beauty and things I've endured. I say wow, it's amazing thank God I'm alive. I choose love. I see me. I see you. The reality of love - it's truer than true. This is where I find more strength in my life. I'm loved beyond the depths of my heart and soul. So - take heart, you reading this, you are immensely loved too. It's simply so.

The things I've learned are too many to name - beauty, strength, and kindness galore. Empathy, compassion, and I too have learned the importance to never keep score. Just be me and shine bright, live my life, and to be happy - even if for that, I must at times fight. The good fight that is, as love is the answer - the strength that is derived from love is profound. It's real strength you see.

A good fight based in love, peace and truth and compassion galore, and what you must learn, don't ever keep score.

Just keep love in your heart, and again and again, you must always stay true.

Be Epic, Choose Love.

Choose love, persevere, choose peace, tranquility and always shine bright, all of this brings such delight. You'll see, do this and you'll be alright. Love - it's such a delight.

Tasha and Weezie and Enzo pictured below, all love and joy. To infinity and beyond, they always know that love is the blessing and what's meant to be; it's about love now and forever to infinity and beyond.

Love it's profound. It's the truest of beauty you see, and all that's meant to be.

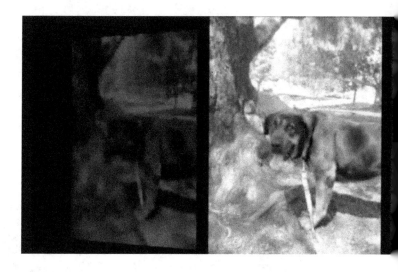

A bad day ..there is no such thing maybe because I don't believe in such things. I know good still prevails every day, every night.

It's true that some days there may be struggle and adversity, just remember with a whole lot of love, and perseverance I say, and a whole lot of hope, all will be okay.

Having a day where you are feeling down? Don't feel your best and you are starting to frown? It is time to turn your frown upside down. There's a secret you see. I can share it, it's also what's meant to be.

There's a very bright light that most hold deep inside, and it's asking you clearly, "PLEASE, don't make me hide," for love is not meant to be kept hidden away.

Love is here to stay, and love never wants to be kept at bay. So today, please choose love for you and all in your view. A kind word or two, holding the door for a stranger or someone you know, encouraging yourself and others too, to make each day special by choosing love in all that you do.

Look for the good, stay strong and be the light - a life based in love, in this gift called life.

Today when I looked in the mirror, I saw eyes filled with infinite love and wisdom looking back at me, filled with tranquility, knowledge, love, and hope, a spirit and soul so strong, composed with love, and so much more.

So many stories to tell, I said who is this woman with eyes still so bright.

I may at this moment feel a bit tired from working so much, some stress here and there, as I advocate for the good in the world to get others to care. The beauty I see, it's profound, don't you see?

It's a life lived with love, truth, kindness and compassion, empathy and a heart and a soul and a spirit based in love - that's strength, with true passion for life.

I stayed strong when I tired, through life's various plights, all through my life thus far every day and every night, for I knew I must fight the good fight standing in peace, and love with all of my strength and might - to overcome all I've survived, to now thrive in my life. Love is the answer.

Be Epic, Choose Love.

I have those who need me to shine bright all of my life.

I have a heart filled with love, it's good and that's right. To the moon and the stars and all the way back, the love each of us has is limitless. Love is infinite.

Bruno and Max, always blessings to me. Love, peace and tranquility. I learned lessons from them, it's for love we must strive for with all of our might.

I choose love in all that I do, not just for me but for you and all in my view.

So today with these eyes staring back at me,
struck with awe saying who do you see? I see me.
I see you. I see love to infinity. I see beauty and
love to infinity and eternally.

Love...

A Gift in This Life

L'amour est infatigable. C'est vrai.

Birds in the sky are beautiful and the free-est of
free.

They live their life with freedom, peace, love and
tranquility.

The freedom to fly wherever they please.

Truly, just like you and me; as each has this freedom, sometimes for some, it's just hard to see.

Freedom exists in our heart and our mind.

The spirit within us wants us to shine.

There's freedom to love.

There's freedom to shine. There's freedom that comes from our spirit, our soul, our heart and our mind, and from above - all of the time.

One's spirit, one's heart, one's soul based in love - it's true beauty you see, that's the truest of beauty and freedom within you and me.

Standing tall such as the Angel Oak Tree.

Able to overcome all adversity, to rise and to stand strong and true, choosing kindness and love in all that we do; love and a life that is true - that is and will be.

49

The beauty we see, which surrounds you and me, shines from within, so bright that it can light up any day and every night. That's freedom, that's free.

The love from within, its true freedom you see.

A choice to love and to be free. We have that ability and choice to make, every moment and each day - radiating from you and from me.

Everyone has the freedom to love, it helps to pray for help from above.

We are all born with the ability to love. If all make this choice to stand with love, it's true freedom you see, and there is a beautiful world which exists for you and for me.

Kindness and peace - everywhere it will be.

If all choose love, it's the free-est of free.

We each have within us a light which shines so bright - and if each of us use it to light each day and each night, we carry that through to inspire others to see - that love is the way and it's the choice that each of us must make.

Love is freedom for you and for me, it's truly for all to see.

I choose love and to stand tall and free.

Kindness and love are beautiful capacities. Standing tall and indefatigable as the Angel Oak Tree, with kindness and love and truth that radiates from you and from me.

All sentient beings - humans and animals deserve to be happy, healthy and free.

Choose love for all, it is what is meant to be.

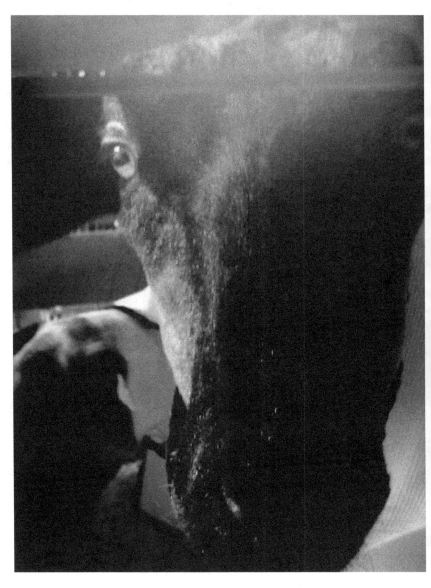

Love is the Way

What do you do when your heart breaks in two -
you mend it, you fix it, you must always stay true.

You reach deep from within and pull from the
strength you once knew. It's still there, it's so
true.

There's a saying they made for both you and me.

A heart can be shattered, quite broken you see,
yet it comes back together to mend even more
beautifully.

Once broken it heals, the truest of beauty comes
back to the greatest extent and the heart
becomes more beautiful to last all throughout life
and to infinity.

You say how do you do that, to rise above from
the pain? Something I've learned ...you do your
best to find the good, and the joy and the love,
and the beauty each day.

Start there and choose love, it helps you to find your way.

Do things you love, be a presence of love, find joy in each and every day. There's always a way to find love and beauty everyday; and pray to God above, He helps us to find our way. There can be rain, a huge storm, strong winds that try to knock us off our feet.

If they do, we still pull through, we stand back up again.

Hold on, choose love, for you too will find your way. The truest of love it's here to stay.

What happens when you have endured storms in life and you get back up, you say?

Well, this time you're stronger than ever before, you may think at times, how can I endure much more?

Yet, the spirit within it's so strong, it remains - you're stronger it's true and things aren't quite the same.

You're wiser, you find so much strength from within, and the love pulls you through every day, you will win. It's the love, it pulls you through, just remember to be your most authentic love-based you.

There's only one you see, just remember to be the "you" God created you to be.

Be Epic, Choose Love.

Rising above adversity, the strength is in you and it's in me. Love carries us through.

How do I know, I live life this way and I know with love we're here to stay.

It's beauty you see, and the truth of the power of love, it's so clear each day.

Love is what is here to stay. When you make a decision to choose love each and every day, this is how you will always find your way. Be Epic, Choose love.

You say, you long for the days of joy you once knew? You profoundly realize the importance of moments so true.

Remember the happy times, joyful memories too, they can pull a person through the hardest of times and get one to happier times - that's also true.

You can continue to create more happy memories. It's true. This happens for me and it can happen for you, and for everyone within one's view.

That's the power of love for all, it's fundamentally true.

The joy and the love it's still present, just choose it, it's true. It's a choice you see. It's as simple as that.

Choose love and you'll see. You will find happiness. The joy it's still present within you; it's a gift from above, it's so true.

I once learned through the struggles that you will still see rainbows.

Glimmers of hope reminiscent of times you once knew. The joy and the love it's still present, it's true.

Struggles and overcoming obstacles, you choose to rise up with joy. The strength is based in love during struggles, and always it's true - this makes you stand stronger and truer than true, by choosing love you too will pull through.

This love starts with me, this love starts with you. It's for each of us who remembers this kind of love, profoundly knowing it's so true.

Kindness, compassion, empathy too, truth through it all with love, you will pull through. The rain doesn't last, just like in nature you see! The storm arrives, yet what does it do? It dissipates after it's through. What appears at various times after the rain and storm's path is clear, the rainbow appears. This is life you see, stand strong and get to the better days that are meant to be.

I once took a trip in a very old car. It would only make it so far. I kept stopping for repairs on this trip that most wouldn't dare in a car I refer to as "voiture ancienne," as that sounds much more beautiful than "old car," don't you think?

So, during the drive, before the repairs, a storm appeared. Visibility was ominous, and the rain was so fierce. The thunder was rumbling and the lightning ablaze. My foot on the pedal - it trembled as the car shook, I knew this was not safe. The storm was so strong, I knew this was not a good place. I mustered my courage, focused and prayed - I stayed on the course and finally pulled off of the stormy interstate. I parked in a space, and gathered myself - and then, I started to pray. It was then I looked up, and turned to the right and the sky - it did part! The side I drove through was ominous still, yet over my shoulder and straight to the right, I saw the sunshine with all it's delight - glistening bright. It's the perfect example of how fast things can change, for the better that is. Just keep the faith!

Love perseveres, that is the truth. Just stay true and never give up. God has a plan for you too, in all that you do.

The truest of true, that's love don't you see, it's God's plan for you and for me.

Love is the message which is so divine, for all it's the plan and how you stay fine.

Choose love.

Remember your worth, remember to stay true. Be your authentic self, choose love, you'll pull through any obstacle presented to you, to overcome - you simply stay true and choose love in all that you do.

The love that is present deep within me, it's so strong - it's so true. It's the beauty of yesterday, today and beyond. You have a gift of love too. It's within you and yours to always choose.

LOVE - It's a gift from above that carries each of us through. Love shines bright, it starts within each of us, it will carry us through.

There's a hope for today that starts within me and it starts within you. It starts within everyone. It's so true.

Remember the love - it always shines through. It's a choice that you make that carries you to ..the days filled with love and beauty galore. You will be glad you stayed strong and choose love just once more, and again and again - and the time after that. You will learn to enjoy life and always pull through, and that - LOVE - it's a matter of fact.

You choose love again and again, you rise up and stay strong.

Love lifts us up, it's present you see. ALWAYS - it radiates from deep within you, from deep within me, and it's present in all, don't you see? Choose love.

And you keep choosing love from within day by day and eventually you learn that the love will always stay.

Love pulls you up from the hardest of times, and then you remember all is divine. For life is a gift of beauty and all of us are meant to shine, pretty much all of the time.

Difficult times are fleeting at best, you and your love are much stronger than that. I know it's true, as it's how I stay true.

There's one little secret that helps you to stand.

Choose love, it stays. It's the way to sustain, even through the most torrential rain.

The love it's divine. It helps one to stand, each and every time.

Love is what gives you the strength to shine and to dance in that rain.

Love gives you the strength to sustain.

Be Epic, Choose love.

The strongest of winds, the rain and a storm -
they are never meant to be the norm.

Love gets you through, it's true, it's the strongest of all.

Keep love in your heart, persevere with all of your might and the storms come to pass. It makes you remember that love is what lasts.

A broken heart can be a thing of the past, if you remember these things and know that your love can endure. Choose love, and don't ever keep score.

There's just one of you, and you are precious too.

Love is a gift from above where you know you can do it, you truly can.

You can stand with love just once more, and again and again after that.

You continue to stand with love in your heart. You remember it's the love that endures, and happier days will reign once more, even better than ever before.

You stand for what's right, you know all that's true - it's love don't you see, it's present within you and within me. Choose it today. Be Epic, Choose Love.

Just choose it today, and each day after that, and live life that way.

You're a special being too, that's true and you are divinely loved through and through, born out of love, which is radiating from deep within you.

Just remember today, and the day after that and always and forever, Be Epic, Choose love.

The love within you has a ripple effect, it starts within and it carries you through, and it reaches all around you, it's so true.

And…. before you know it, you exude love in all you do. Others become inspired too and they too will remember to choose love in all that they do for you too - and all in their view.

The love carries forward and it helps you stay true. Kindness exudes and you help others remember that they can stand tall too, they remember to choose love and to always stay true.

That inspiration started with you. It started with me. Love is so beautiful, it can help all to see - that the truest of beauty within you, within me, it's all based in love.

It's choosing love starting with you and for all, don't you see? Love exists for you and me.

Perseverance and strength starts from within. Remember your worth, it's what you know that is good and much more than that.

You find love from within and seek the good all around you, love is so strong it carries you through. That love carries forth and you find inspiration in you.

Love has a ripple effect and helps others to see.
Love perseveres and it comes from within, God
placed it there to help you to see all of the beauty
that is meant to be.

Love - it's a choice and a gift from above given to
you and to me, it's given to all, don't you see?
Love is a gift from above. It is truly what is meant
to be.

That love carries forward, it carries you through,
before you know it you inspire others to choose

love too. Others too need love to stand tall, to push through adversity, rising above it all.

You remind them it's true - a beautiful heart, soul and spirit based in love, shines the brightest through it all. Love shows you beauty each and every day.

You remind many others to persevere with love ..it's the way.

Choose love everyday, it carries you through to even brighter days.

Remember your heart once broken in two, it started to mend, that started in part because of the love found within you. Choosing love in all you do, it carries you through.

The shattered heart, it mends it's true.

Choose love. My heart has been broken more than a time or two, yet some may say, with one's heart still hurting today, how will I ever find my way? How do you heal, they may say? How did it happen? Just choose love you say? Yes, choose love, start with you, radiate love in all that you do. You will inspire so many around you to heal their hearts too. I know the truth, and it's simply divine. Just light up each day with love all the time.

I'm shining my light, lighting the way, helping others to find their way - to step away from the darkest of days.

Choose love, shine bright, remember the path of love, and truth and kindness, that is the way. You say you are feeling a bit grumpy today? Why should you smile, you may say? I'll tell you why. A smile will warm up your heart all of the time; and for another, a warm smile could be their actual lifeline.

Be kind, a smile can help one take heart, and help them remember that there is love in this world, and that smile can be the start. Your smile is a work of art, God made it that way. Just remember to use it today. Light up the way. Create a path of love today. You can choose that today. Be Epic, Choose Love.

What about the broken parts in one's heart you may say, I'll tell you, I know the truth.

I can confidently say, choose love. The broken parts, they come back together even more beautifully. A broken heart heals with love. Love is the way.

Think of this today - you say your heart is shattered, and your heartbreak is profound, KNOW that when you choose love, your heart heals with empathy, kindness, grace, forgiveness, and compassion. And, that's just the start. Love - it's healing your heart today. Continue to choose love, starting with you and all in your view, and the love will stay.

Your beautiful heart, it will heal and become even more beautiful with each passing day.

Be Epic, Choose Love. Love is here to stay, just make that choice today and every day, for love - it's here to stay.

The saying I mentioned in this very verse, a heart on the mend is even stronger you see. For the broken parts once healed, they mend even more beautifully. The joy you once knew, where is it you say? It's there, you can choose it today, just like love it's here to stay. Another blessing that's true, the joy you once knew - once you heal, you will realize it grew!

Love is a gift from above and it's here to stay.
Choose love, you will find your way.

A broken heart mends with love which starts
from within. Love is a beautiful gift from above.

Know your worth, it's based in love. You will
learn what's beautiful and oh so true, and you
will continue to choose love in all that you do.

Why does the heart mend more beautifully? You
had a choice and you chose love you see. You are
reading this book today, take heart - that's a
start! The love it's meant to be. You chose it
today. Keep choosing love, again and again, and
you will see the most beautiful you come back
again. You are already beautiful, and by choosing
love - you know it's true. God created you.

Stay true, choose love again and again.

Love repairs the most broken of hearts.

Using wisdom and knowledge and the love from above and within, to heal the pain felt so deep, you realize the choice you must make - it's the love you must keep.

Be Epic, Choose Love.

So you reach deep inside for the strength that is there. You see beauty where some wouldn't choose to care. You say look at the sky, and say wow, it's so stunning today. I'm blessed for this life, those are things you might say.

How do I know? I've been there you see. I found the love deep within me, it's so present you see.

It's there for each of us, love is present in you. Love is present in me.

It's a beautiful gift from above, quite divine. Choose love; you will see ever so clearly and beautifully, all of the good that exists and all of the good that will be.

And you stand with love in the best of ways - for
the good, peace, compassion of all, as well as
always knowing that love will prevail.

To rise above pain, you realize you are not the cause of your broken heart, it's about learning and living, you live and you learn..

you rise, and you love. Just remember to choose love and always discern.

Shine bright, overcome those obstacles with all of your might, and you choose love and you prevail because you must. I choose love. Love - all can trust.

Choose love today, and you too will realize that love is here to stay.

Some just don't get it yet, they don't realize true strength.

When there's love and compassion, that's truer than true. Love is the strongest of strength, don't you see?

Love is present within me and it's present within you.

Love is the utmost strength, which carries one through, it inspires many - starting with you. The love within, it's pure beauty, it's true. For you are of love, love carries you through.

So the beauty you find each and every day, it fills your heart up with blessings galore.

You then realize and profoundly know that there is so much more good in store.

The love others lack for you or for me, it's not about us, they are just hurting you see. The love within you, and within me, it's from a pure heart based in love you see. This ability is a choice all can make.

Love is healing for you and for me, and all who you can see, and those who you may not yet see based on one's proclivity. Choose love. Love is an ability of which all have the capacity, all can choose love today.

Be Epic, Choose Love.

Love's light shines so bright, it's blinding to some, it hurts their eyes for a time, so bright that they can't clearly see. The beauty is love. Love - it has the ability to shine very bright, choosing love and kindness, with all of one's might can help others to see and it can eventually give them much needed sight.

Those who are blinded by the bright light, as we shine with our light based in love so bright. They may try to see with all their might, yet they can't see the love within you, or within me to the clearest degree, because there is a message that they must first learn to see - their own worth and beauty, their love deep within starting with them - then they will see the love that radiates from you and from me - and also from them.

The love is present within them too, they just need to learn how to clearly see.

Be Epic, Choose love.

Choosing love in all we do, all can learn to do this too. Choose love.

There is a saying you see, which definitely rings true.

Shine your light so very bright to help others to see that love can radiate immensely - creating a world of pure beauty, love, peace and tranquility.

When one chooses love and joy, it will be.

Once all find love from within themselves, they too will see so very clearly. All must choose love too from within, and then they will see that love paves the way to all that's meant to be - a life filled with beauty, hope and much joy, peace and tranquility.

Choose love, it's there and starts from within. Love carries us through and the pain it will heal.

The love from within which comes from above mends the heart.

The shattered heart is now mending you see.
Love carries us through, it's within you and me.

Always choosing love starting with you,
remember it will carry you through, and it will
inspire many others to choose love too.

The brightest of days so beautiful and bright,
that's the hope of the now and the future and
how it's meant to be, in all its delight.

Choose love. Learning one's own worth is a
priority.

The love that you find which comes from within,
it has a beautiful ability to bring the happiest you
back again.

Now with wisdom and truth, love and knowledge
and strength realized, the most shattered of

hearts fill up with love. The kind that goes from this page to one's heart, to remind many that love is there, there's always plenty of love; so do not despair, just remember - Be Epic, Choose Love today.

Love doesn't deplete, and remember, love comes from above. It's a gift for you and for me, and for all, you see.

Love is a gift from above, a beauty capacity that helps one live a life of beauty, joy, peace, grace, and tranquility.

Love is what is meant to be.

So remember what's true. It's the love that radiates from deep inside of you.

It's important, it's true, love carries you through.
Stand strong based in love and overcome strife in
this life, to go on to inspire many, you see. Love -
it's meant to be.

When you choose love in all that you do and
remember the joy and the love found within you,

and within me, and all in one's view, please know that is what is meant to be, and the truest of true.

The beauty and the love, it has always been there you see.

Love is meant for you and me, and every living being to perpetuity.

Now, and forever, to infinity and beyond, love can always be found.

Love is here to stay, you need not look far away. Start with you, you have love you see, just choose it today.

It's always within - within you, within me. Love is within every being you see.

Love is a beautiful capacity.

Love helps you to see clearly and realize all of the good that's meant to be.

Be Epic, Choose Love.

This is Truth

Life, how I know it's supposed to be, is a series of beautiful moments, moments become memories to always cherish.

There are times in life that we long for what used to be, the friendships that at least to me, I thought would truly always be.

Life brings some valuable lessons, at times some of the truth and reality of the current state of the world isn't what we hoped it would be.

Tears stream, when in one's heart it seems that the world could be filled with more love, kindness, truth, compassion and empathy, for all sentient beings - you see, love IS what is meant to be.

Love, it exists always, yet one realizes as a society all aren't yet where we need to be, where we ought to be. We can get there as a society when we all choose love. Love is the most beautiful capacity.

There are times deep within I cry for society, for all human and animal injustice, it's not how it's meant to be. Suffering is caused by a man's proclivity at times to not choose wisely, or kindly or from a pure heart based in love.

When will it get to the way it's meant to be, to stop the suffering, to stop the cruelty - suffering isn't the way the world is meant to be.

We must all choose love. Choose love today. It can help you find your way, and it is this way for all others too, just remember to choose it in all that you do.

Love is what's meant to be, for all to clearly see. Choose love and all will see all that is truly meant to be.

There are love based possibilities, it all starts with you and me. We can all choose love to infinity.

Please be kind to all, to see a world filled with love and tranquility.

Be a presence of love in a world filled at times with too much hostility.

Love is needed for you and me, and for all, you see.

Be epic, choose love always, for that's what's meant to be.

The innocent animals suffering is a travesty, people go hungry because the greedy think there isn't enough for you and me, there's more than enough don't you see?

All - every human being and animal, those who you see and who you don't see, based on your proclivity; all deserve happiness and to be healthy, and to be treated with kindness, love, compassion and empathy. All deserve to be free. Love is freedom. Freedom is love.

Be Epic, Choose Love.

The truth you see, there's a beautiful world
which exists for all to see, that is what's meant
for you and for me; and for every living being,
those who you see and who you don't see - based
on one's proclivity. We should all recognize that
all sentient beings need love and deserve love.
And, all still need you and me, everyone you see,
to choose love.

Love, it is what's meant to be.

Find love in your heart and be love, choose kindness for all you see.

Stop suffering for every sentient being, suffering is not meant to be.

Be kind to all, human and animal, it's what's meant to be. Choose love.

Choose kindness and love and you'll heal your own heart too, just wait and see. It's what is meant to be.

Suffering takes a toll on humanity. Face truth, and rise up with love and truth, and kindness and empathy to take a stand against adversity.

Stand for a better world with love, to stop the cruelty. What affects one, affects all you see.

A love based world and love for all will heal all of humanity and all sentient beings in the world.

Love is the choice to make for you and me, and every living being, you see.

There's a new found hope waiting for all to see. Choose love in your heart and rise up against adversity.

Rise up to stop the cruelty, the world is not beautiful for all, but it most definitely can be... when all choose love, don't you see?

Choosing love starts with you, it starts with me and starts with all as far as one can see. Love matters for every living being in the world truly, not just you and me.

Love for all is truly meant to be.

So much suffering in the world and that's not what is meant to be.

Love will cure humanity.

Stop the cruelty.

Choose love, it's not just about you and me, it's about every living being who you see, and who you don't yet see. Be Epic, Choose Love.

Every living being matters. Innocent beings are not meant to be suffering.

It's time to wake up and face reality.

The world is harsh at times and that's not what is meant to be. Too much suffering which not all see.

Why compassion and empathy? ..those are things we need..you see.

Choose Love.

Stand strong with love for all, it is what's meant to be.

Choose love for all, it's what's meant to be.

Love can change the world for the better for all you see. Love is truly what's meant to be.

As a society we realize what truly is meant to be, it's love indeed - I hope all take heed.

Love must prevail for every living being, not just you and me, or who through your perception you see.

You matter, I matter, every living being - the ones you see, and who you don't see; all of us, every sentient being, matter immensely to infinity...

Love, peace, compassion, kindness and empathy is important for all in the world, and it will be.

Choose love today.

Man needs to unlearn his selfish ways and return to love. It's a right for you, it's a right for me. Love is a right for every living being.

123

Choose love for you, for me, and for every living being.

Love is what is meant to be and in the world - this is what we are supposed to see. It's not supposed to be filled with so much cruelty. Rise up. Stand up.

Shine your light bright.

Choose love.

With love and kindness, each of us can choose to be a part of creating a world that's meant to be. A world based in love, that is what is meant to be.

A world that is not filled with so much hostility.

A world that makes things better for not just you, not just me, but for you and me - and each and every living being you see. A world with utmost love, that's what is meant to be. Wake up to stop the cruelty.

Be Epic, Choose Love.

Do not choose apathy. Love must take a stand today and everyday, to create the beautiful world that's meant to be. All beings - human and animal, each and every being in the world, those who you see and those you don't see based on your proclivity, all deserve love.

We must live in a world which is meant to be. We must stop the atrocities. We can do so by always choosing love.

Choose love for all you see, for human and animal, love will be and is meant to be.

Create a world meant to be. Rise up, choose love and stop the cruelty.

Be Epic, Choose love.

It matters for you and me and every living being you see and every living being you don't see.

Stop, don't turn your back. Nice poetic prose and lyrics you say, but already, unless the words sink in you're on your way...apathy - it's definitely not the way. Choose love, love is here to stay and it's the only way.

Please allow the words to sink in. Turn around. Listen to the words I say.

I speak the truth, don't walk away.

The words I say, I need you to hear them today.

Wake up, turn around - please

don't be a clown in a world that needs you today - to choose love.

You? Yes YOU. Everyone gets a say and you, you have a choice to make today.

Be Epic, Choose love.

Rise up, stand up, don't look the other way. Stop the cruelty, speak up against atrocities. Stand strong by choosing the strongest of strength - that's love, be kind, who are you I say?

Choose love. Be Epic, Choose Love - you are needed today and everyday to choose love.

Start with you, please choose love in all you do, this love will reach all in your view, it's so true.

Love and kindness, it conquers blindness. The blindness I speak of is not in the physical sense, it is the inability to see the love. Love is there, it starts with you.

Shine your light, stay true and help others to choose and find love too.

A strong person is one who stands with love, compassion and empathy, and who does not look the other way.

Be Epic, Choose Love.

What is strength, it's love I say. I know the answer, first step you don't look away and please listen to what I have to say in this verse today. Remember love, it helps you to find your way.

Choose love and kindness each and every day. Choose love, it is how we find our way.

Love is what is here to stay.

Stand up today, choose love, please don't look the other way.

Kindness can and does exist in the here and now today, if everyone would just stand up and say, I choose love, this is who I am and who I am going to be today and everyday. I choose love.

Beauty

There's beauty that is present each and every day, please remember to see it, let nothing stand in your way.

It's present, you see, in the here and the now. It's within you and me, and as far as the eye and the heart, and the soul and the spirit, can see.

A beauty so profound it's present today, when you choose love, the love and beauty is real and it's here to stay.

You wake up and see the tallest of trees, a colorful sky, or feeling a fresh breeze. There's beauty in that, simply profound - yet what some may call simplicity.

The simple things in life aren't simple at all.

They are beautiful, inspiring, profoundly a gift. The tree over there standing so tall, sustaining such wind at times when you think it might fall.

...The breeze that you feel on your skin and the fresh air during spring, summer, fall and winter, it's not simple at all.

These are profound gifts of living and of life, there are too many to name, too many to count. The beauty of nature, each day so unique. Once living in Palm Springs, walking in the warmth of the sunshine, yet not too far away one can see a snow covered mountain peak glistening in the sunshine - even during a winter day.

Wherever you live, there are blessings you see, this life is a gift, nothing so simple, it's all quite profound.

True beauty exists, it's all around.

So much beauty is present, it's all based in love, truly gifts from above. The steps you take, the words that you speak, the air that you breathe, plant based foods that you eat, and the water you drink, the smile from a person on their lunch break;

every friend, every dream that you dream in your sleep or while awake, there's too many to name. These are blessings you see, way too many to count in actuality. The blessings are there abundantly. It is the blessings you must seek, and you shall never be weak.

The gifts in this life are abundant, you see. My point is simple yet so profound, never focus on strife. This life is a delight. Choose love each day and all in the world will be alright.

There may be struggle and pain at times in this life, this is true, yet put your focus on all of the good and the love that shines from within you. Then look around at this beautiful world with a grin. There's so much beauty you see and often it's found in what some may refer to as simplicity.

The gifts of this world and the beauty of life, serve to remind you not to focus on strife.

Love more, realize that love is true strength, it's all a delight. This enables us to know that life is meant to be beautiful and happy, filled with peace and tranquility, the truest of love.

So please don't focus on strife and be sure to treat others right. Choose love and compassion, true empathy too, for you and all others for kindness matters for all in your view, that means you too!

Choose Love always, it's what we must do.

Be Epic, Choose Love.

True beauty you see is found within you and within me, it's a decision each day to choose love everyday, there's beauty in that for all who can see.

Shine brightly, choose love, see the beauty galore. Learn to never ever keep score. Keeping score you might ask, well what do you mean? The answer to that is quite simple, you see. Strive to be the best you that you can be, and stay true, choose love, shine bright for all to see. Never compare yourself to others, that's not you. The gifts are infinite for each of us you see, just be the best you that you can be, and choose love.

That's true beauty, you are the only you, don't you see?

God just made one of you, and that is a gift, born into this world to inspire and uplift.

Start with you, your love must stay true. First start with you, when you choose love and kindness starting with you for yourself and clearly see the good found within, you will easily choose love and kindness for others too.

Realize all in this world, born out of love are here for a purpose which comes from above. How do you find it and how do you see all of the beauty which surrounds you and me?

The answer is clearer than you may currently see. Choose love for all, that starts with you. If painting or dancing or singing rings true, or if writing each day is in your heart, you must do this, do what you love, that's a very good start.

Choose love and kindness, starting with you. Do you remember yourself as a young child, what was it that you wanted to do? Teaching or writing or playing the sax? Does a walk in nature inspire you too? Often our purpose is easy to see. Start here, as a child what did you desire to be?

Remember to stay true to your authentic personality. Be kind, uplift, choose love for all including yourself, and do what you love, for in our hearts we have the ability for joy and happiness which truly comes from above.

Remember to proceed in this life as a peaceful dove.

A pure heart is something which we must not lose track of, for within each of us there's a love so divine, for it comes from above, and then we realize, all in this life can be as peaceful as a beautiful dove.

Love is a gift in this world, a gift to see and from which all can appreciate and experience so much beauty and tranquility.

Often adults get hurt in their life, due to some strife, then they put up a ruse; forgetting to be the truest of true, which of course is the love based you.

So, I say this to you, remember to honor the child you once knew and in terms of this, I'm speaking of your inner child, that's you.

The child within, the one you once were, the one who knew to never keep score. The truest of you and the purest of heart, remember that's you, the one you once knew. Honoring this is the key to the happiest you - just remember, stay true.

True joy, love through and through and a beautiful heart that's the true me and that's the true you, that's truly all of us who are born of love. We all have this beautiful capacity to love, it's true.

And by this I'm stating, remember to stay true, keep your authenticity in all that you do. Choose kindness, choose love. God only made one of you, honor the child who was once you, the child within, that's you. The one with heart and compassion galore, it was when you were a child, you knew to never keep score.

My point is this, the joy you once knew and your beautiful pure heart too, I'm speaking to the inner child who exists within you; to this - you must always stay true.

Don't let the strife of the world tear you down, you're a child of God, and that is profound.

Your beauty and love with a purpose divine, you're meant to live life with love all the time.

Be kind, lift up, be the truest of true, the authentic love based you - it's so beautiful, it's true.

Remember I said don't ever keep score, it's true
you see, there's no need to be like anyone else,
we all have gifts and blessings galore.

God made you unique and there's just one of you.
You are special too you see, composed of love,
just remember to be the best you that you can be.

Choose love and compassion and the gifts are
profound, you'll soar through life with true
beauty in leaps and bounds.

The beauty and love it's easy to find. It
profoundly comes from the divine and it's within
me and it's within you, truly for all - it's true.

Choose Love, just be the most beautiful love
based, you.

Just as the sun rises and sets with beauty galore, you were created perfectly to radiate beauty like that and even more. I know it's true, I see it in me. It's why I can see it in you, and all in my view. The beauty and love it's truly there. It's so true.

Live a life based in happiness, and choose love and kindness for every being that you see. Lift up and encourage, that's needed today.

See the beauty in each and every day, in each and every way, please choose love today.

Realize when you always choose love, it's here to stay. Choose love each and every day.

Love and beauty starts deep within, consistent each time. Just remember of course - you came into this world straight from the divine.

So you must remember to lift up and inspire, choose love and be true, this is a message for all of you.

By choosing love, you love a life you profoundly desire.

The beauty, it's present in each day you see; that's because it starts within you and it starts within me. Beauty is present in every living being you see.

Choose love and kindness in all that you do, that's the beauty which radiates from me and from you, and from every living being, every human and animal too.

We are born from love and we all must stay true, choose love and kindness for all starting with you and everyone else, for human and animal, every living being matters too.

The world needs love, choosing it for ALL is what each of us truly needs to do.

Be Epic, Choose love.

Meant to be

Love is something that is meant to be. My question is why can't everyone see? This is beauty to me, the strongest of strong, choosing love is what is meant to be.

At times there can be heartbreak in life, some forget to choose love through all of the strife.

The hardest of days, love still exists - the important reminder is to always persist. Not all do this, many resist.

Why do you think some find it so difficult to choose love each day? It's always there, pray they find their way.

Love is there for all you see, when you stay true to your heart, you can realize all that is meant to be.

Struggles in life - they are present you see - however in each, there is an opportunity to grow and to flourish, to rise above all adversity, to shine bright using your God given gifts to rise above every obstacle you see.

Choose compassion and love, starting with you, it is what is meant to be.

The love starts with you - you find it within, the tears will subside and the love found deep inside, always found from above, it must win.

Heartbreak is real, many feel it you see. You must learn to stay strong through the pain of heartbreak.

Choose love just once more, again and again, one day learning to dance even in the most torrential rain.

Life should be lived to the fullest - there are blessings each day for this life is a gift. Please don't be foolish. You must realize this.

I'll say it again, this life is a gift.

Life is a gift, stand strong and say, I will live my life to the fullest each day.

I choose love for me, for you and all in my view today and everyday. I will lift up and inspire, choose kindness for love is the way, for the love - it must stay.

Those who speak unkind things, they are hurting you see.

They haven't yet realized that love is the way. Love starts from within, you choose it and then it will stay. Love is a choice, you must choose it today. Love should take precedence and it's what is meant to be. It truly is the way.

I know what it feels like to live life to the fullest - surreal moments in time occur when one is most true, sharing the joy and love found deep within you.

Then the happiest of moments are created in life, they become true. Life feels like a dream - a joy and it's true, it's because you choose to be true, starting with you.

You choose love and joy and then beautiful moments in life present themselves, it's true. This joy and love is representative of the very best you.

It's the truest of true. It takes strength from above and found within to stay the course, for that is true.

The joy and the love, you find it within you.

You pray to God for help, to see the way to the happiest and most beautiful you. This happiness radiates from deep inside you and inspires all of those around. This is beautiful, it's true.

You can live life with a heart, and soul and spirit based in joy and love and kindness, in all that you do. Love is the way, remember it's true!

You can wake up excited to start the day and know in your heart of hearts that nothing will stand in your way - a life to be truly lived with happiness, joy and love, the life you must lead for yourself and all who you see.

Choose love - it is what is meant to be.

I say to you, please always stay true.

The question I have for you is, are you living the life that is the truest and happiest for you and inspiring all in your view to choose love and happiness too?

You have one life to live, you must always stay true and choose the happiest and the best you. The authentic you, the one that is love based and true.

Remember yourself as a child born into this world…

When you choose joy and love each day. Go as far back as you need to, when you remember feeling joy and love profoundly. Remember this joy and love today. Decide to bring it back, and you can trust, it's here to stay.

Then move forward in life choosing love and kindness, starting with you and all others in each and every way.

Start there, for it's love, empathy, joy and kindness and compassion and a heart that is pure, that brings beauty galore.

Add to that true wisdom - knowing that love and happiness matters immensely in this life, this helps you to always remember to stay true and to soar and overcome strife.

Choose beauty today, choose love, that is the truest of you, the one that stays true, the one who inspires every being around you - to also stay true and choose love, it's something we all must do.

Others insecurities, which others may try to push on you, remember they just haven't yet learned to stay true.

The love they see in you, they need to find it for themselves, it's true. If they can't see the beauty in themselves, it's hard for them to see it in you. There is healing they need to do starting with them.

This is why you must always stay true, choose love for them too, for love heals you see. Even if at times it needs to be from a distance maybe, love perseveres, it gets all of us through. Just make sure you are being treated with love too from those in your path. If not, stay true - continue to choose love in all that you do. Choose love and kindness for them and one day they may choose love too.

Love it inspires, it is something that all truly desire.

Love is what is meant to be for you and for all you see, and those you don't see. Love for all is meant to be.

Love starts with each of us. So if you already know the profound blessing of finding love from within - starting with you, you must shine your light bright. You can help others to choose love by shining bright and choosing love with all of your might. You can most definitely help them to choose love too.

Don't ever take heed of other's words said to you which are untrue or hurtful, it just means it's about them, simply put - they have some healing to do. They must first find love from above and from within starting for themselves too, so that they can proceed with love and kindness for themselves and others too.

Unkind words stem from unhealed hearts and at times insecurity, so pray for them so that they may find true love for themselves too. Sometimes the love one has for others, helps them to see what is most beautiful about themselves. That is what it is supposed to do. Then this love will radiate for others also. We must be kind and love based with ourselves to have this ability to inspire love around us. So remember to be kind and love based starting with YOU.

All have more healing to do every single day, but what heals a heart is realizing love is meant to be and it is here to stay. It's why one is certain to choose love each and every day.

For the strong we proceed with love, we uplift
and inspire; we don't tear down others, for there
is no desire.

We choose love, and kindness. It's the strongest of strength, so pray for those still healing so that they may find their way to what is meant to be.

Of course, it's love you see, for all, every living being, human and animal as this is what is meant to be.

Love is a choice, choose it today, for you and for me, and for every living being you see and for all in the world, this is what is meant to be, of course it's love, do you see?

It's the truth, love - it is what is meant to be.

Others insecurities come from hurt you see and they cannot yet realize all that is meant to be. This is why you choose love for you, for all you see; for every living being, you and me, and everyone, human and animal, those who you clearly see and those who you don't see.

Love, compassion, empathy, kindness and truth, it's what is meant to be.

Live your life with joy and love, explore each day with the peace of the dove.

Shine so bright that others may also see their way to realize that love and beauty is the way to be.

Kindness galore, it definitely helps others to soar.

That's each person's responsibility to choose love, this is what is meant to be.

A warm smile to each you encounter, this has the ability to help heal a heart. You don't believe it? Be kind to yourself and others, choose love and kindness always, and you will see.

So wake up each day, let nothing stand in your way to feeling love, joy and peace today.

The naysayers may say, why are you so happy? Your peace, your compassion, the joy of a new day.

They may ask, What do you know which they have not yet realized based on their proclivity?

Don't worry, just lead the way. A bright light shines, as it helps others to see that living life with enthusiasm and joy today and every day, it most definitely is the way.

Live your life, this life is a gift. Choose love and live your life to the fullest each and every day.

Love and joy, surreal moments in life based in love and tranquility, I know this is what is meant to be; for all, human and animal, for you, for me, for all who you see and those who you don't see. Love - it is what is meant to be.

Those moments in life where all is sublime - it makes each of us remember, we are a direct extension of the divine. That is why each and every one of us is meant to shine.

Know this, today is the day you can live your life
with joy and sunshine.

Do not focus on the strife, put your focus on
realizing the beauty and love within this gift
called life.

Love is prolific. Life is a gift, see it for the truth of
this and you will appreciate it in all its delight.

A Man I Once Knew

There was once a love that I believed would be,

The kind which stays true, the truest of true,

One that prevails above all adversity.

Two people who could truly see the immense
good in each other, and all that's meant to be.

A moment in time, decades ago, they would
meet, and in one's heart with the truest of love
you believe, and think that this kind of love is
meant to be.

Life takes its toll, yet true love perseveres, and it
does so in the heart and in the mind and in the
soul, and all that we know.

Communication - try as we may, the beauty we
felt, so true and so real -

The kind of love that you know will stay.

Yet to this day, the toils of life try to make it fade away.

A real love, the kind that no matter what others think or what they might say - in your heart it's a love that will stay.

Communication kept at bay, a lesson to learn even to this day, choose love always in each and every day.

For with even a love so true, that we once knew, it led to broken hearts, where is the love we once knew to be so true. Communication is essential, without it - the love, it can fade. Sure, it's still in the heart and the soul and the spirit, but love is a verb, if you don't speak or say how you feel, you can't hear it.

The sunniest of days we would have, with a love felt so true. One doesn't question, maybe as much as we should. What felt like moments that would last for all time, have become a distant memory.

It's just like a flower, so precious and true. I say to you - the one I loved and once truly knew, when you didn't stay true in what you would do, as I always did or would try to, it's true...

When you turned your back on the love you once knew, and didn't seem to care to be there and be true, with flowers you know, they need proper care to grow. When you turned your back on the love you once knew, you neglected the one who always has cared about you.

You turn your back and how does a flower grow, they can I suppose and in fact, I know that to be true. I still did you know, I kept the love I had for myself to continue to grow.

A love felt in one's heart, without love that you continue to show through actions of caring and thoughtful communication and presence of heart, when you seem to have forgotten these things of the love you once knew, the relationship just stopped. You didn't stay true, to me or to you.

That was up to you, to be there or not, but somehow I seem to be the one you forgot. It was up to you to keep or to lose the love you once knew.

The beautiful flower, who cherished the love felt for you - you simply turned your back, it is true. The beauty that remains is this - the flower she didn't ever wilt or fall apart, some do, losing a love so true. She took heart, and kept the love in the heart she once knew not just for you, but for me too.

The beautiful flower… the miracle is, she still grew.

Who is the woman you once knew, you knew that the love was so true. You see this is her story, it's true. The beauty within her heart stayed true - even through her heart breaking in two, quite shattered it's true. You didn't step up to be the man she once knew - that was up to you.

Why did this beautiful woman with a heart so divine continue to be mostly fine, whose smile can melt all of the ice of wintertime, who persevered and stood by your side because she still saw your light, that you held deep inside?

She continued to stay strong, and choose love you see. For her, love didn't waiver, it always stayed true - it's consistent you see, the way love is always meant to be.

Much more than a love she thought was meant to be - a love that you know which can overcome all adversity, one you feel deep in your heart and your spirit and soul. The kind of love that you know will survive, it's true you see, the love I felt for you, and for us, I saved enough for me, it carried me through.

I filled up my heart even more - a miracle it's true, love perseveres. I already had this love radiating from me, so when you broke my heart in two, quite shattered it's true - it hurt, it's true, but what could I do? I had to continue to choose love you see, this time for me and for all in my view, and in my heart, soul and spirit I continue to choose love for you too.

I had to remember that I have a love much deeper than I truly realized, found from within. I often prayed for help from above, I would continue to live life with the peace of a dove and a love like no other. The love that sustains the greatest of wind. It's the kind of love which makes you go in and out of my life and back again and again - getting me to believe that all of the love that I felt and could see ever so clearly - is what was meant to be.

The girl you once knew, who truly loved you, the one that you loved, her love was so true. She's consistent you see, the love that she has, it's what is meant to be.

So you see, when you turned your back on me, not measuring up to the man I knew you to be, and could be, when she needed you to be a good man to me, and to truly see all of the good that was meant to be, she realized that with or without you, a love she adored, she would stand up tall and give it her all, not faltering once and she would choose love just once more, and again and again for love is the way... and I knew in my heart, the love it must stay.

This time the love that you once knew was so true, the joy she exudes, the brilliance, the humor, the many things that make up the girl you once knew - she's unique you know, one of a kind, a beauty so true, a smile divine - a heart filled with love, strength based in love and the peace of a dove, a smile that shows how bright her heart, her soul and spirit truly are in all her delight, that girl you once knew with love so true...

When you turned your back on the girl you once knew, she still stayed true to the love she knew. I had to keep it for me, it's profound and so true. For the love that she holds, that you knew was so true also for you, she kept it you see, for it is always within her. The love you chose not to continue to see, thank God I kept enough for me.

So I took my love and healed my own heart, for it was always there right from the start, and those of us meant to shine, we always will, you see. This time instead of choosing you when you weren't there, I chose me. The love from within, praying for help from above, I kept it you see to rise above all of the hurt and the adversity. I stayed true to the girl you once knew, I'm consistent you see. She's still here, here for me and here for all who can clearly see. Choosing love, it's what is meant to be.

When I needed you most, you didn't stay true.
You turned your back on the girl you once knew -
that wasn't me, that was you, at least for a time
you forgot about love or caring for me, it's true.
See - love is a verb. Love starts in the heart - but
it's action you see. You turned your back on me,
that's not what love is about.

I had to stay true.

The love we once knew, between you and me,
well I'm not sure you see - meaning it has
nothing to do with me, when based on another's
proclivity to not choose wisely that they let go of
a love that I thought was meant to be.

What is up to me, it's to always stay true, as I
always have, you see.

When a man does not follow his heart, well he could lose the love of his life you see. How do you get this back? You choose love and all that's meant to be.

Choose love for you, a healthy love, one that is true, kindness, compassion, empathy, truth and real love - the kind which is so true. The kind you took from me, the kind I gave to you. How I sustained, how I flourish even in the rain, how you turned your back causing me pain, I didn't lose my love, for my love sustains. I choose love, you see, that starts with me.

The love you took from me and couldn't reciprocate freely or with true strength which is love - the love you must find within - start with you and then maybe one day you can learn to stay true, apologize to me for not staying true, and for not choosing love for me and all that was meant to be. Choosing love it's what you were supposed to do. You couldn't see - for had you found love within, you could clearly see all of the love meant to be and you would have shared that with me, the one you once knew, whose love you took so freely.

I believed in you and me, I believed in a love that was meant to be - the love I learned it was largely coming from me, for love is a verb, it's an action you see - one based in love, kindness, communication, empathy and seeing clearly all of the love that is meant to be. It carried us through, you see.

For without my heart and love so true, I would have had nothing to do with you the first time you broke my heart in two, quite shattered, it's true.

I've learned, it's true, that the love deep within my heart and my soul and my spirit, it stays true and it always remains. Perhaps why I never found blame with you, I knew in your heart the love was true, and through some actions too, and the fact remains my love is true. In fact, with you and me, I carried us through. The love you lacked for me in your actions, it's true, I made up for two - what I always have had for me and for you, that is why you didn't have enough love to carry us through to be there for me, as I stepped up for you. I needed you to be the man I knew you to be, so I had to learn to be there for me, you set me free and choose foolish ways, foolish I say because it is foolish to keep true love at bay.

The love that I have it's the truest of true, I am the girl who you once knew, and who you loved, I knew, and who is truer than true. This kind of love you once knew. You let it go because you first had to find it in you.

If you have love which stays true, you would realize your wrongs and say sorry, it's true. You would become the man I thought I knew. You would pick up the phone and say - it's me I need to talk to you today. At least be a friend to the girl you once knew.

You'd decide that you would learn to stay true - you would be there for me as I always was for you. You'd say sorry for all I ever put you through, I should have been there for you in so many ways it is true. You'd say to me, I deserved better from you, it's so true. And, you would finally stay true, and become the man I needed you to be, the man I once knew.

You would learn to be a man who chooses love, the one I once knew, new and improved choosing love, it's true. You would realize how profoundly you hurt a girl you once knew. You broke my heart, it was shattered, that's not all from you. Life takes its toll, I rose up from the pain, this is not about blame, this is to say what's true, I needed so much more from you. You hurt me, it's true, I just wanted you to step up for me and be true to me, the girl you once knew, who truly loved you too. I do know you loved me too, you just couldn't be true and that is about you, you had some healing to do. We all do it's true, yet some of us stay true, and for me, from you, it's something you didn't do.

I want to say check your ego at the door, I'm not worried anymore. But I'm not placing blame and no I'm not worried, but my heart is not in a hurry to forget about you, I am not sure I ever want to. I choose love, I have learned to always throughout my life, continue to choose love once more and again and again.

Love is the way, I know it must stay. And so it remains. Love is a choice you see. Love is an important choice to realize all of the love that is meant to be.

Choosing love for me and all in my view, I send love out each day to create a beautiful world. I know heartbreak, I know pain. I know how it's important to stand strong and learn to dance and even find joy in the rain. I reached within, prayed for help from above, to keep the love.

A life based in happiness, peace, love, tranquility, empathy and compassion for all living beings, I choose love.

I always did you see and always will choose love. I just didn't have enough for both you and me, when you couldn't see clearly to be able and willing to choose love for me. It is what was meant to be.

A real relationship is based on reciprocity, once you find love from within your own heart, soul and spirit, then a love meant to be, will be.

For you see, a good man takes heart, he is there for the woman who was there from the start, whose love stays true. She chooses to stand strong with love throughout her life, she is a work of art. She chooses love. She didn't and doesn't ever fall apart. I choose love, which leads to a beautiful life, from which a man with love in his heart, doesn't depart.

You may stumble and fall, for you don't know it all, none of us do you see.

Yet when you stumbled and fell, you hurt me. When you stumble and fall you must learn to get back up you see, don't follow the way of foolish proclivities.

You knew from the start, the beauty of all that was meant to be, but for some reason you couldn't share all of it with me. I was there for you, everytime you needed me.

Life is full of choices, when you base them from a foundation of love, which is true strength, you can recognize all of the beauty that is meant to be.

You hurt me you see, where is the man I once knew - who has a light which shines bright too - when you choose for others to see. You stopped sharing it with me - you fell to selfish proclivities - you are better than I know that to be. Much better, don't you see. If you truly understood all of the love that is meant to be, it would be.

The flower you neglected and pretended you could no longer see, she continued to shine bright in all her delight, knowing all of the love that is meant to be, it must start with me. So when you couldn't see or stand up to be the man I needed you to be, I just reached deeper for the love which exists in me. I know how to be present with love for me and all in my view, for those who know how to choose love too. You didn't see. You didn't even choose to be a friend to me. I know at the time you couldn't see ever so clearly.

The flower you neglected years ago, she decided to choose love, she stood up and grew. Well, what do you know?! She found strength deep inside, a strength to which you didn't learn to stay connected. Love is so true, it starts with me, it starts with you, each living being is created from love and stands the strongest of strong with love, it's true. Well, thank God I grew, with love so true.

Thankfully I had enough for me and for you, and for many in my view, just to simply stay true - to proceed with love, compassion, truth, joy, kindness and empathy and kindness too, in all that I do. I pray for help from above, it's so true. I rose above and decided to stay true, and the love I have remains is true blue. Remember to follow your heart, stay true and choose love, joy, kindness, truth, empathy, compassion and authenticity in all you do.

Be Epic, Choose Love, it's the truest of true.

Gratitude

I am truly thankful for so many things. A foundation of love, moments of joy, compassion, empathy, kindness and truth, and every new day, is a gift, it is true. I'm thankful for the ability I've shown and have, and that's the ability to love and to do my very best to choose love in all I do. The ability to love from a pure and good heart right from the start, starts with each of us.

Seeing the beauty that surrounds each of us is a gift. Life is a gift, each and every moment to be cherished and when we proceed with love and kindness beginning with ourselves -we then have a beautiful ability to radiate a presence of love for others too. Through love and kindness, there is an ability to lift the spirits of everyone we meet, human and animal.

I'm so thankful that I remember to see all of the beauty in each and every day. I stop what I'm doing, the days when I can, to see the sunset and I rush if I have to, to make it in time! I know appreciating the beauty in each and every day is so important, there are gifts all around. Remember to cherish each moment. Choose love for all. Life is a gift. Every moment is precious - choose to live life that way and it's true, I'll say it again, then the love - it will stay.

All of the photographs in this book are from living life, and all are original photographs, most of which I took even before I knew I would ever publish a book!

Be Epic, Choose Love.

Be kind. Then life is divine. You'll feel better, you'll see. Love makes a better world for you and for me.

I'm thankful for love. I'm thankful for the gift of life. I'm thankful that I choose love, always have and always will. Love, compassion, empathy, kindness and truth are beautiful gifts and things we must choose to live a life of all of the beauty that is meant to be.

Be Epic, Choose love.

Words of Love

Enjoy your day everyone and through this gift of life, live your life authentically, and choose love in all you do. Love is a beautiful gift from above too.

Love is present in every moment of everyday life because love starts with each of us, and love is a beautiful ability that we all have and can choose to perpetuate in each and every moment of each and every day, choose love.

Shine bright with love, as we are all meant to do.

Be Epic, Choose Love.

About the Author

Lisa J. Pellegrene is an American journalist and publicist, a 20 year strategic consultant for filmmakers, philanthropists, entrepreneurs and artists, a TV film professional who has worked as talent on national television, to include the Travel Channel, and as a producer and writer for various TV and film productions. She is an animal welfare advocate (rescuer and vegan) who advocates for love and kindness for all. She is a social justice advocate, who is also an ambassador for Rise and Stand advocating against bullying. She is a woman who stands strong with truth, compassion and empathy, kindness, hope and love and who knows the importance of love for all sentient beings, human and animal.

She is the Director of a forthcoming re-launch of a project that she conceptualized entitled, "Peace, Love, Unity Dance Troupe TV," she believes in the uplifting and inspirational power of inspiring music and dance and knows that everyone, (human and animal) has gifts and talents to utilize to make a positive difference in the world based in love.

Her first significant role on national TV as talent was when she was featured on Travel Channel's "Top Ten Southern California Beaches," where she spoke about the beauty of Catalina island and swam, kayaked, and also snorkeled in the Pacific Ocean surrounding the shore of Avalon Beach of the island. This program aired nationally for more than ten years on the Travel Channel. She co-founded "Pittie's Angels," truly with her dog Pittie who inspired the awareness group, speaking up with love and compassion for all animals and especially those who are at times unjustly discriminated against. She is a freelance journalist, whose articles have been published in the media sources such as Broadway World, Asbury Park Press (a USA Today affiliate), Chicago Tribune, LA Weekly, and on Patch in various cities as a contributor, to name a few. Advocating for her clients through her publicity work has led to national television appearances, and inspiring stories that Lisa writes on behalf of clients, which are published in national and regional media publications.

She is a lifelong advocate for love, compassion and kindness for all sentient beings, human and animal, by example.

Beautiful Pittie and Alex, they are love through and through and huge blessings, it's true.:)

Author "Be Epic, Choose Love" - Lisa Pellegrene

She is a supporter of many animal welfare organizations such as Sea Shepherd, Best Friends, Animal Defenders International, various farm animal sanctuaries such as the Gentle Barn, Farm Sanctuary and Woodstock Sanctuary that she supports through her advocacy and awareness efforts to further promote various organizations that are making a significant difference to create a better, love based world for human and animal.

She is a peacemaker with utmost strength, which is based in love, kindness, compassion, empathy, truth, and perseverance. She chooses love.

(Pictured with Sea Shepherd, at a VegFest in the south) - Summer 2018, showing support for the outstanding human beings who are doing their part to make a love based, epic difference in this world for all sentient beings.

Twitter and Instagram @lisapellegrene.

www.officiallisapellegrene.com

Stay tuned for additional volumes, the inspiration stays true and I have many more inspirational epic lyrical poems and poetic prose to share with all of you.

Remember, choose love for it sustains, it's how you make it through the torrential rain. You just don't sustain, you rise up to see - a need to be epic by choosing love, peace, truth, kindness, empathy and kindness for all in your view - that means for you too!

Be Epic, Choose Love.

CPSIA information can be obtained
at www.ICGtesting.com
Printed in the USA
BVHW040442230422
635157BV00003B/3